TRUTH SET MET FREE

David Bartholomew

Copyright © 2025 by David Bartholomew

All rights reserved. No part of this book may be reproduced or transmitted in any form or by any means—electronic or mechanical, including photocopying, recording, or by any information storage and retrieval system—without permission in writing from the author, except in the case of brief quotations used in reviews or articles.

Scripture quotations are taken from the **New King James Version®**

ISBN 979-8-90046-968-3

Staten House Publishing

DEDICATION

I want to dedicate this book to my Lord and Savior, Jesus Christ, and the memory of my Father and Mother (Bill and Honey), My Wife Sherri, my Daughter Angela, and her husband Ryan, as well as All My Family

I have decided to write this book because many people I have talked to over the years have suggested I write about my life. I named my book Truth Set Me Free because everywhere I go, I hear the question, What is truth? It is my hope and prayer that by reading my book, you can also learn the truth.

I grew up in a family where I was the oldest of four boys. I want to honor my mother and father. We lived in many homes growing up and have had many experiences that helped shape our lives, some for the better, and some that left us with broken hearts and a need for healing. As I looked back on my life, I can see how the Lord has had His hand upon all of us.

I am in no way blaming my parents for any hardships I had to endure while growing up because, as you will soon read, things have happened that were totally out of their control, and as an adult, I now know they had no choice. To us, it was about survival and finding ways to keep us all taken care of while circumstances beyond our control unfolded. I also would in no way change my growing up because it brought me closer to God.

I am putting my life out there for people who have struggled all their lives because of the way they grew up in unstable homes and needed a Savior. I went to church as a child, but it wasn't just about a God I couldn't relate to until one day, God brought me into a relationship that completely changed and healed me. This same experience and relationship are for everyone —ask Him! His name is Jesus! Even today, at 70, God is still setting me free in areas I didn't know I needed to be set free! I want to start this book by introducing my mother and father, who had a big influence on my life. They raised four boys and gave us a foundation that would one day lead me to grace.

A Letter to the Reader,

    Dave is a Godly man of faith and caring. As you read this book about his life and growing up, you will see "that" in his character. He wasn't born with a silver spoon in his mouth, but he achieved what God wanted him to, and that was helping to raise his own siblings and bring peace and sanctification to the prisoners. He answered God's call and went to prisons for many years. Sometimes, though, scary situations occurred, but he endured and never gave up. Thanks be to the man of faith that he is.

    We will never know how many men were saved by his answer to God's call. His reward is waiting for him in Heaven. May God richly bless him as he continues preaching and shares the word of salvation and truth to all people.

    I know you will enjoy reading his life story. You'll be anxious to find out what happens next, so you won't be able to put it down! May God richly bless him for giving us a blessing and encouragement.

From,

    A very Caring Friend

CONTENTS

Chapter 1	Mom's Story
Chapter 2	Dad's Story
Chapter 3	Growing Up
Chapter 4	There Is A Marriage Coming
Chapter 5	Panic Attacks Begin
Chapter 6	Moving To the Mountains
Chapter 7	Getting Saved
Chapter 8	The New Life Begins
Chapter 9	Moved Closer to Church
Chapter 10	Getting Equipped
Chapter 11	Stepped Out Into Construction
Chapter 12	Teaching Job at Career Center
Chapter 13	First Mission Trip to Saltillo, Mexico
Chapter 14	Mission Trip Two - Another trip to Saltillo
Chapter 15	Third Mission Trip - Last Trip to Mexico
Chapter 16	Fourth Mission Trip - Off To Venezuela
Chapter 17	Prison Ministry
Chapter 18	Men's Group
Chapter 19	Retired and Moved On
Chapter 20	Surprise Blessing From God

CHAPTER ONE
Moms Story

Mom had "Rheumatic Fever" as a child, and the damage wasn't exposed until the 1950s when I was born. This was the beginning of my mother's heart problems. Being a devout Catholic, she continued to have more children despite the doctors' warning her not to have any more. She had another son ten months later, then another son a year later, making three boys. She lost a couple before having the fourth son, nine years after my birth.

When I was nine and my youngest brother was born, my mother began to get worse to the point that she was hospitalized for a month at a time. That's when my siblings and I began living in separate homes.

As time went on, Mom's heart was going downhill. But she never gave up on Jesus. She talked about her love of Jesus all the time. One night, my youngest brother, who was five at the time, came out of her bedroom, where she slept and spent most of her time. My baby brother announced, "Mom's dead". The first thing I thought was, how could my little brother know Mom had died? We ran into the bedroom and sure enough, no pulse, not breathing! Because of what I learned in Boy Scouts, I immediately raised her legs on a pillow, then gave her mouth-to-mouth and began CPR. My brother called 911 —or maybe someone from the funeral home 11 miles away, since it was the only ambulance service around. It took a long time before they arrived, and the whole time we were waiting, I was doing CPR.

Mom survived, and I believe we didn't see Mom for six to nine months after that. She spent those months in the hospital. Shortly after the incident, she had a new valve put in her heart. We stayed in two different homes, split up as usual. This really put fear in my life because we never knew when she was going to die again at home.

Mom and Dad always wanted a daughter. Sherri and I married in 1974, and in 1975, we had a daughter. We were able to bring her to the hospital a month before Mom passed. Mom got to come home for a couple of weeks, and she got to babysit for about an evening. My brothers were there also. Angela, being the first girl in the family, got a lot of attention and love. Everyone wanted to hold her and take care of her. Mom had the time of her life with Angela. That's all she talked about for the next week. I never saw my mom happier in my life, and it brought joy to all of us to see her that way.

Later in the month, Mom returned to the hospital and began getting worse by the week! Her doctor said he was going to try to put her on a heart transplant list. Sherri and I spent 8-hour shifts with her sisters for three days. Sherri and I went down to the chapel at the hospital and asked Jesus to take her home to be with Him. When we went back up to her room, the nurse said, Your mom just passed on to be with Jesus. She talked about Jesus all the time, and now she is with Him. It was extremely sad, but Sherri and I were thankful she went in peace, no more suffering! We knew where she went! Mom was a very loving and kind person. She had a lot of fear, probably from being so sick and in the hospital so much. I remember the day of our wedding, her legs were so swollen and leaking fluid from heart failure, but she made it to the wedding! She never gave up on Jesus!

CHAPTER TWO

Dads Story

My father, Bill Bartholomew, served in the Korean War. Mom said that, with years of struggling, Dad fought with much anxiety from his time in Korea. We found a card in his military papers that listed his name, indicating he had served with the Golden Dragons Special Forces. Dad would never say a word about the war until he was about 60.

Mom and Dad, as I stated earlier, married in 1954 and had me in 1955. They went on to have two more sons within 25 months, and after nine years, there were four of us. Dad used to lie on the floor at night and, with two hands and one foot, move our cribs until we fell asleep. Dad seemed to spend most of his free time in a doctor's office or at the hospital seeing my mom. I don't really remember spending any time with him until we were teenagers. He loved baseball and used to play with us. I remember him watching baseball on TV at times.

Dad had been frost bitten in Korea, and his hands and feet would crack and bleed in the winter. He told us when he got older that the Chinese chased them for three days and nights in the winter, and when he got back to their tent hospital, there wasn't much skin left on his feet. He suffered with that for many years. I remember that Dad had to hitchhike to work a lot because he always had old, unreliable cars. He had a good job, but he had to pay the people who watched us, and hospital bills also took up a lot of his pay. The neighbors and friends of my dads would often bring us food. I remember when I was a teenager, he was so upset because St. Elizabeth Hospital in Youngstown, Ohio, said they had to release Mom because they hadn't received a payment. When her doctor found out, he went in and took care of her bill. It felt like we had to act like grown-ups from about ten years old, and we didn't know what to do the right way.

Eventually, after my mom passed away, the hospital filed charges and put a lien on our house. They were demanding full payment for her bill. Even though Dad had good insurance, his hospitalization coverage would expire after reaching a certain amount. The hospital took Dad to court to sell the house. Sherri and I paid off the lien and made the repairs necessary for us to live in the house. All my brothers came to us and wanted Sherri and me to buy the house to pay off the lien. We gave him the mobile home we had in a local park. Not long after buying the house, we filed a hardship case with the township, and they permitted us to move the mobile home down on the property where the house was. After about ten years, Dad decided he wanted to move into housing for seniors, where he did well, after spending over ten years living with us before wanting to go on his own. We still took Dad everywhere we went.

I must tell the story about Dad babysitting Angie, our daughter. One day, we came home from work, and they were both in his jeep in the backyard with the windshield wipers on because my youngest brother had a goose that would chase him. They were afraid it would get them! The goose kept going around dad's jeep and wouldn't let them out. That's what dad said.

Dad loved all the kids; he would play kickball and interact with them as much as he could. They referred to him as "Mr. B". He was loved by everyone who knew him. Nobody was a stranger to Dad. He loved fishing. One time, he caught a big Walleye and left it on our porch wrapped in a bag with ice while we weren't home. He was a giver. Probably his greatest attribute was to surprise and bless everyone else! If you were at a wedding and he was there, he would out-dance everyone and have the whole place laughing. When we went anywhere with him, we saw everyone laughing and saying, "Here comes Uncle Bill, look out!" he should have been a comedian. I just loved being around my dad; you couldn't be down when he was around.

My dad's cousin Rudy used to fix our TV when we were younger and still at home. One day, he brought it back after repairing it and plugged it in, and smoke came out of the top! No more TV!

Dad and Rudy went fishing a lot when they got older, probably in their sixties. On one of their adventures, Rudy was backing his truck up to unload the boat into the lake. Come to find out, he forgot to put the plug in the boat, and it was half sunk before they got it hooked back up and pulled out of the lake! It was quite a fiasco because Rudy started having chest pains when the boat started taking on water, and they had to call an ambulance.

In conclusion, Dad gave his life to the Lord shortly after we did and often attended service with us. This really changed his life for the better. He was under so much stress when we were growing up because of my mother's health. Now, he was set free and had so much peace and joy.

One Sunday, Dad arranged for me to preach at the apartment building where he lived. While I was preaching, I looked up at him and saw tears streaming down his face. I was so taken aback that I almost started crying myself! I never said anything to him, but the Holy Spirit was loving on my dad.   God is totally awesome!

One more story about Dad. When my daughter came to visit with our grandkids, we knew they would bring squirt guns, "Super Soakers," and my Dad would hide with the garden hose, and anyone in sight was going to get wet. We laughed so hard when they came over!

CHAPTER THREE

Growing Up

I was the oldest of four boys. As I mentioned before, our Mom had a bad heart, and between the ages of eight and ten, her heart started giving her trouble. My first personal memory dates back to my first grade. Mom sent me to school with a little bottle of medication, which was clear. I can remember the teacher not believing it was medication because it was clear; my Dad even had to go to school and verify the prescription. I remember it was something that would calm me down from anxiety. Now, I cannot recall if it worked.

My Dad was forced to put us in places where people offered to let us stay; most of the time, we couldn't stay together. I remember being in fear a lot because we never knew where we would be living. We often stayed at our two aunts' homes, off and on. By the time I was ten or twelve, we began spending more time away from home. The year I was twelve, Mom had a mitral valve replaced, and we didn't see her for about nine to twelve months.

We were scattered around the neighborhood in New Bedford, Pennsylvania, and parts of Youngstown, Ohio, at our maternal aunt's house for about seven years. We didn't see each other that often, but one time, Bob and I stayed at my aunt's house in Youngstown, Ohio, and she let us smoke cigarettes; she even gave us a whole pack. She made us promise to never tell Mom or Dad. It was our secret, she told us. She said, "You kids have seen enough, you need a cigarette! We jumped on that! Now we felt grown up at around thirteen and fourteen years old!

It is always a joy to share the stories of where we lived: some good, some bad. One place we stayed, my youngest brother was four years old, I can only remember his age because he didn't go to school yet, the mother beat him so badly that he had blood under the skin from his behind to almost the back of his knee. We couldn't tell Dad because we seemed to be gone when Dad came to pay them to watch us! We decided not to tell Dad because we felt sorry for our Dad! I had to hold a lot of stuff in as a kid. My other brother argued with her about what she did to my younger brother. She made him leave that night. And go to where our other brother was staying. Thank God he had a place to stay with the family my other brother was staying with. To us, that was just life, but this one hurt me badly. I was just 14 years old, and I felt helpless and had no one to talk to. Back then, you respected adults regardless of their actions. This was a different situation, and I didn't know how to handle it. So, like everything else, I stuffed it inside and would cry at night when no one could hear me. I stayed at that house with my youngest brother for over six months. It's hard to bring that story up again!

One family, who kept us the most, had five kids of their own, who were the same ages as each one of us. This place was our favorite place. We all loved being with this family! We built strong relationships with each other that still last today. The relationships with this family were rooted in God's love; their parents instilled many Godly principles and a strong work ethic in all four of us.

The father managed a farm at a Catholic Convent that supplied beef, pork, and eggs to the convent and also to a large hospital in Youngstown, Ohio. Everyone who lived at their house worked on the farm every day. After school, we gathered eggs from two chicken coops, which housed 6,000 chickens. We fed 75-100 cows and 200-600 pigs. This is where we learned how to chew Copenhagen! Wow, I got sick a few times, but we didn't believe in quitting—not very smart—but we thought we were as grown-up as adults.

On Saturday, we shoveled manure and cleaned the pig pens, both inside and outside. There were four open pens for hogs of different sizes. We also ground feed and cleaned the egg grading room. We had to grade the eggs seven days a week.

We all went to church on Sundays, and the rest of the week was just a normal day. We had so many good stories when we lived there. At the farm, there was a convent and a private girls' school for girls from all over the world. We would all look out the bedroom window at night and look down at the dormitory and talk about the girls we saw while working on the farm.

This was where I first got my hunting license and a shotgun. I'm just guessing, but I think there were over five hundred acres of land, so we had a lot of land to hunt on. The Dad there kept my shotgun until we could go hunting with him and his boys. This was our second home, but when we got to go there, it was home! We have been friends with the three boys and two girls since 1967. I have so many memories, and I could write about them all day!

At the age of fourteen, I had a cyst on my side. I was put in the hospital and had surgery on it. I spent a month in the hospital because they felt someone needed to monitor me, and there was nobody at home to do that. Two weeks later, I had surgery again. I am sharing this because I had only one visitor in one month. I believe all these things caused so much grief for my father, who never gave up on us. Back then, we thought this was just life, but it takes a toll on our feelings. Also, we always felt protected; after getting saved, I realized it was the Lord's protection all along! He will never leave you!

Shortly after I turned fifteen, we got to stay home and live in the house by ourselves. Mom came home from the hospital for about two months a year until I got married, then it was about one month a year until she went home to be with her best friend, Jesus. Mom and Dad always got along when they were together. We always felt sorry for Mom and Dad; he stuck with Mom to the end and taught us Godly principles: respect, how to take care of each other, and always saying yes, no, thank you, and may I please! I am thankful for the time we had with Dad, even the short time we had with him as a child. Dad always took me with him to visit sick people and to funerals. Dad had a lot of respect for people, and it taught me to be the same way.

My brother Bob and I both had several small jobs cutting grass and delivering newspapers, and I also had a paid job at the farm from the ages of fifteen to sixteen years! I've got to say, the man we spent time with and worked on the farm really taught us how to work! When I reached 16, I got my license and a better job.

We had one car in the family for years. I bought one when I turned 16 from saving money for a couple of years. Dad's car always seemed to break down, so I would take Dad to work after school, then go to where I worked, which was a couple of miles away. I would get home from work at 12:30 am, then get up at 2:00 am, drive fifteen miles to the bakery, pick him up, and go back to bed till 6:00 am for school. I don't know how we ever did it, but we just had to do it to survive. We did this for about six months in my senior year of high school!

Dad bought a used Volkswagen Beetle. Bob and I would take it to the laundromat on Saturdays. Saturdays were Dad's day off, and he usually slept a lot on those days. I was in the driver's seat, where I worked the gas and brakes and pushed in the clutch while Bob shifted the gears and steered the car. We drove like that for nine miles on the back roads to the laundromat. We would switch on the way home. Those were the days! No matter what our situation, we always knew how to have fun and push the envelope, so to speak! I must tell this story. When it snowed and our roads were always the last to get treated, we used to hold on to the bumper and drive down the road, then slide on the snow or ice! That was really clean fun!

The neighbor next door worked at a steel mill, had a small farm, and had a wife with three girls. We were up at their place a lot and helped him with all his chores. A lot of times, he brought a dozen donuts home from work and made sure to call us to come up. He introduced us to putting peanut butter on glazed donuts. They were delicious, and we still eat them that way when we get them!

The rules in our house were that the only places we could go were school, work, and the neighbors, because we had to look out for our younger brother, who was nine years younger than me. So, we could have friends over, but we had to be quiet and out of the house so Dad could sleep! We always played some ball, backyard football, baseball, or kickball. Using the house as a backstop for the catcher. The back wall was where the bathroom was. Our neighbor used to always remind us about the time when the ball went through the bathroom window — yes, and you guessed it — out the window came Dad's head, yelling at us in a scary voice. To this day, I don't know anyone who could yell like Dad could, and I'm sure we deserved it! The neighbor said he knew we were in big trouble that day! We used to reminisce with our neighbors and friends about those Golden Years! When I look back and think of all that we went through, I can't believe we made it out okay! As those years went by, we had many more stories to share —like any other family, some you share and some you don't!

I was about to graduate from my High School Career Center, taking carpentry, when I met a neighbor girl on the bus, Sherri. Her sister told me that Sherri wanted me to ask her to the prom. She lived a quarter mile away from me, but we never really knew each other because we either worked or stayed home because of the rules. We went to the prom and hit it off well! We started dating, and we were only allowed to go out one night during the weekend and visit one night during the week! Being raised with mostly all boys, this was new, exciting, and scary!

CHAPTER FOUR
There is a Marriage Coming

Now at the age of eighteen, I realize I may have met the love of my life. Sherri is a redhead and full of life. We dated for a year and a half. I proposed to Sherri on the first Christmas. I worked as a carpenter, helping to build houses. I got laid off for a week and went to sign up for unemployment, and was offered a chance to get a job on the Railroad as a bridge carpenter. I got the job, and a couple of months later, Sherri and I planned to get married in October at the ages of nineteen and twenty. Sherri and I planned our wedding and had a reception at the fire hall. Sherri's Dad wasn't coming to the wedding until that very day! He didn't want to lose his first daughter; I can relate to that now! He showed up and offered us his new truck to go on our honeymoon! It was a great wedding and reception. Sherri's family brought food, and mine did too.

*So, I have to tell another story....*We got married and went to stay in what we call the mountains. The next morning, we went into town for breakfast. When we came out of the restaurant, a police officer was standing there! He said, "I'm going to arrest you for parking on the wrong side of the road! I felt like we were in a Backwoods movie where they threw you in jail! I looked at Sherri and said, "This isn't good. I think I'm going to jail, along with some other thoughts! All said and done, we just got a ticket! Of all things, my father-in-law lent us his truck, and I thought they were going to impound it. Knowing my Dad and what he might have said, I was scared to death of telling him, but it turned out okay!

We both came into our marriage with some experience. Sherri was the oldest of five siblings, and I was the oldest of four. We both played a big role in raising our siblings! So, we started working and learning how to be husband and wife. We lived in an 8 x 30 camper trailer for one month and then moved into a big farmhouse a month later. We had a terrible experience just a month after moving into the farmhouse. A cousin had accidentally been killed in a gun accident at our house while we were all sitting at the table playing cards. This was devastating for the whole family! We started off our marriage with some sad problems!

Then we moved again because the heating bills at the farm were atrocious! Thanks to my father-in-law, who had a friend who sold mobile homes, we purchased our first home for $ 5,000. We moved into a trailer park and lived there for nine years.

Sherri became pregnant, and she was sick every morning! She came into the bathroom losing her stomach, and I did right along with her! Those were tough mornings! We went through a lot as everyone does. Eight months later, we welcomed our precious daughter, Angela Marie. Thank God for putting us together. His hand was on our life and marriage from the beginning. Angela came home from the hospital sick and returned for a week, then came home to stay, weighing only five pounds. While she was in the hospital, a very close cousin of mine was her nurse. God puts the right people in the right place all the time, and we don't see it until it's over. Thank You Jesus!

We were able to take Angela to see Mom while she was in the hospital. And she laid her on her chest. Mom was in bad shape at the time, but she lit up when she saw Angela for the first time. Mom got out of the hospital a couple of months later. She was able to watch Angla for an hour with my brothers' help, and that was the first time I had ever seen her so happy. We all cried with joy that day! Angela was a beautiful baby, and we loved her every day! Shortly after we took her to see Mom, Mom's health went downhill fast. She went back into the hospital, passed away, and went home to be with her Precious Lord Jesus! It was a tough time for all of us; we just never thought she was going to pass, after all the times she died and came back.

We met a girl while living in the trailer park, who became Sherri's friend for over 50 years and remains so to this day. Her Mom and Dad looked after us for several years and became lifelong friends until they passed away. Her friend played a big part in our lives some 20 years later. At the time, though, they took us under their wing and helped us in many ways. They became another Mom and Dad for us! What an awesome couple to steer you in the right direction.

At that time, we are coming into winter. I was working on the railroad, and Sherri was a great wife and mother, keeping the house going and working full-time at a dinnerware plant, decorating dinnerware and commemorative plates. It was a cold winter, and we had problems keeping the water lines from freezing! I had to get up an hour before going to work, thaw out the water lines, and work on bridges in wet pants. I gave up and installed brand-new water lines inside the home, then covered them with wooden trim boards.

The problem was that we began heating with wood, so there was no heat on the floors where the water lines were. We have many great memories of living in the trailer park. They were kept spotless back then. It truly was a whole new life raising a daughter and learning how to be married and new parents all in ten months!

CHAPTER FIVE
Panic Attacks Begin

Shortly after Mom went home to be with Jesus, I began to have panic attacks. My brother-in-law came over one night, and I had to go into the bedroom because I was too nervous to sit and talk to him. I put up with this for a couple of weeks, so I went to the doctor. I had arranged to come to the back door at the doctor's office because I had so much anxiety I couldn't wait in the waiting room. I went to my Mom's doctor. He told me that if I kept this up, I would make myself sick. He put me on nerve pills, and it made it worse, so I threw them away. I started drinking wine to calm my nerves! I couldn't even go into a store by myself without having a panic attack, and I left the buggy in an aisle and left the store.

Before all this, I never had a problem with getting nervous! I used to go into the hospital and see my Mom with wires and tubes all over her, and it never bothered me. I could go and stay at anyone's house, and it never bothered me. I always had joy in my life, but I had a real heartache for what Mom and Dad were going through! It all started right after my Mom died!

One day, while on the railroad, we were told to go home early because a winter storm was about to hit. I was driving home, and you couldn't see the road due to the snowstorm. I saw red lights barely flashing up ahead, and I stepped on the brake pedal; the truck went sideways, heading right for the guardrail. I knew where I was, and if I had hit the guard rail and gone through it, it was a long way down, and I would have been killed. I jumped out of the truck just before it hit the guardrail and landed on the road. Bad move, but fear will control you if you let it!

Another good story for you is one about a winter when I had a pickup truck that wouldn't start when it got cold out. My Father-in-law came and pushed me down Main Street with his wrecker, as fast as it would go, and in the end, you must go left or right with his wrecker, as fast as it would go!' After the truck started, he kept pushing me until at least 50 mph before the Y, where I had to turn! For several months, I told Sherri 'I think your Dad is either trying to kill me or preparing me to drive a stock car! He built stock cars and Harley-Davidsons and raced them. Well, I lived through that situation! So many stories, and I'm sure you all have stories of your own!

    We used to get together quite often on the weekends with brothers, their wives, and friends. One weekend, we were going to order pizza, drink some beer, and have a good time. My wife ordered the pizza, and the other women went to the bar to pick it up. After about half an hour or so, and they weren't back yet, we decided something must have happened to the car, so my brother, I, and a friend went to the bar to see what was happening. When we arrived, two guys were kicking our friends' car and wouldn't let the girls leave. My brother and I jumped out of the car and started fighting with these guys, and one guy yelled, "Shoot them, shoot them!" My brother and his friend jumped in the car and left. I turned around and saw a girl with a shotgun just twenty feet from me, and the guy yelled to her, "Shoot him!"

I heard the click from the shotgun, and she cocked it and the shell ejected, and she did this three times, and none of them went off! They jumped in the car and left. My brother and his friend came back with guns and saw their truck, a hundred yards away, at a beer, wine, and produce store. A cop pulled out of the store and was chasing them. The cops caught the girl, and the guys fled on foot. The guys had just robbed the store. The cops came to our house later that night to take a deposition from us, and we never heard from them again. God spared my life; it had to be a miracle for that gun to misfire three times. I didn't realize God saved my life that night until after I got saved.

    We continued to live in our hometown for about ten more

years. Sherri went back to work to help with the finances. I would get laid off for two months every winter for about five years, then I worked full-time from then on.

Gotta Share a Story! When I worked on the railroad, we worked on a bridge job for six months, and one day, a Drifter was getting water from the river to make tea. He stayed in New Castle for the next six months. He was all over the country and had many wild stories to tell.

I got to meet so many people from all walks of life who made an impact on my life. I worked with nine guys and a foreman, and after seven years, the railroad combined three gangs into one in the Ohio region, retaining nine of us, including me. It was a dangerous job, and four guys from our original gang went on total disability with back injuries. They had equipment for us to use, but our foreman made us all work by hand, changing ties and steel in bridges.

On weekends, we would go camping on Sherri's parents' property in a small camper with our daughter and the two neighbor girls, who went everywhere with us. Their Dad was a bad alcoholic, and we wanted to help them from abuse. I still drank, but the kids never saw me drinking. It helped calm my nerves, but only temporarily.

One weekend, we had our daughter, the two neighbor girls, and their 4-year-old niece. Well, the gnats were bad when we got there, so we built a fire, and it began spreading immediately. We rode the 4-wheeler down to my in-laws' spring and filled a 5-gallon jug with water. There wasn't enough water, but the fire went out on the road! Then we got together, and the little niece was missing! You talk about panicking!!! Well, we found her in the camper a couple of minutes later! So we all loaded up, took the kids to our favorite spot in the creek, and got cleaned up. These kids never gave us any trouble and became lifelong friends with our daughter and us. Always something, but we loved it!

About two years later, I injured my back at work and didn't file an accident report, so I was on my own. Shortly after that, the railroad began abolishing the rest of the gang. I tried working on my own, but the pain in my back stayed the same as time went on. We talked about moving up to the mountains. So, we put our house up for sale and looked for a house up there. My brother lived up there, and Angie had just finished school for the year and was getting ready to attend a new school for 7th to 12th grade.

CHAPTER SIX
Moving to the Mountains

We sold our house in my hometown and bought a house in the mountains. A camp that a college professor had. It needed a lot of work, and I had the time now. The setting was beautiful, with a creek nearby the house and a spring on the property. We remodeled the inside, but I had help from a friend I met there. My back was still too bad to do any heavy lifting or to bend over for long periods. We were only about three miles from Sherris' Mom and Dad's camp. It was on a dirt road that led to probably more than 100 camps down on the Allegheny River.

We met many people heading to their camps. The first year, there was a drought, and many campers heard we had spring, so we gave everyone permission to get water. This led to many parties on the weekend and too much drinking. I still had panic attacks frequently, and drinking seemed to help.

We saw a lot of wildlife in the area, including a bear that visited our garbage on Sunday nights before Monday pickup. Sherri was nicknamed Annie Oakley! My Dad spent years with us there. A couple of times when I was doing a small job somewhere, Sherri and my Dad would go, and she would get a deer, in season! We had a lot of good times up there as well. Well, Any Oklie shot a bear one season, and we ate the meat and made a rug out of the pelt! What an exciting day that was! We harvested deer and turkey living there. An awesome place to live!

Gotta Tell Another Story! We were having a party at our house, and several family members came and stayed. We went to bed, and I woke up with something landing on my face. I grabbed it, threw it, jumped up, and turned the light on, and there was a snake at the foot of my bed! I hit it with my shoe, and under the bed it went! I told Sherri that if we can't find that snake, we will burn the house down! (Fear speaking there!) We found the snake, and I killed it. Needless to say, I slept in the truck that night! The reason I was so scared is that I had been talking to an Amish guy about a month or two before that, who had timbered a lot of woods right where we were, and he said that area was full of Copperhead snakes!

Back to our daughter and her struggles! Angie was a good runner throughout school. She used to beat all the girls and boys throughout school. Devastation hit again in our family. Angie came home from school one day and said, "I think I have diabetes". We said, "Why would you say that! She said she was listening to the radio, it was diabetes awareness week, and said, "I have all the symptoms!" She was getting up at night to drink a lot of water and couldn't get enough. We made an appointment with her doctor. When we arrived, he asked Angie what was wrong, and she explained the situation. He said, "Don't think that is what it is, but we will take a test right now. He came back into the room crying and said, "Your sugar is extremely high, go to the hospital right now! We all had to take classes on type 1 diabetes before she could come home! She was in and out of the hospital for a year; they called it brittle diabetes! She eventually did a good job managing her sugar intake and even became an excellent baker. She had to give up basketball and became a cheerleader!

Gotta Tell This Story! When Angie graduated from High School, she bought a car. One morning, she went out and started it; she was scared in the dark because of a bear. She came in to let it warm up, then she went back out. The car was gone. She came into the house screaming My Car is gone! When I ran outside, the car had rolled down the hill almost into the creek! It was never a dull moment! Angie graduated from High School and went to college to study nursing.

Back to the chores we had there. We had to cut a lot of big cherry and red oak trees off the property so they would not fall on the house!' Gotta Tell Another Story', There was a hermit that lived near us who had a sawmill that ran off an International 4x4 truck front axle. He lived in a shack and did a good job forecasting the winter weather. He was over eighty years old and could work like a fifty-year-old. My father-in-law lent me a 100-foot cable and two pulleys, and we cut down over 20 trees with our neighbor's help. The elderly man's name was Tutor, and he helped me load many trees over a period of a year, and he cut them into 1x6, 8, and 10 inches at his sawmill.

 One day, when he came, Sherri told him I would be home from work soon. She said the bottle caps were blowing off the top of his home-made beer. He would come every day until we loaded all the trees and took them to his mill. What an amazing man he was! A real legend, and he loved Jesus! Those were the days!!!
  We used the cherry wood on the property to build new kitchen cabinets. I also built a dining room on the porch that was there. I also built the cabinets and installed the cherry wood walls. It came out nice.

         We also cut a lot of firewood to heat our place, and we always had help. The whole family helped from Grandpa to Angie. Even the neighbor helped! We did so much together. Those were the days. I look back now and can't believe all we did, and I kept the anxiety to myself and masked it with wine. This was starting to stir in our hearts, and we didn't know what it was. Too many parties and drinking started to increase, and I didn't feel like we were going down the right path.

As time went on, Sherri and I continued to feel the urge to explore some churches in the area. One Sunday, on a cold winter day, we had a flat tire on our truck, over 15 miles away from home. I had to change the tire, so we missed the church service. We couldn't seem to find the right church for us. We had been attending a Catholic Church for most of our lives, off and on. Just going through the motions, thinking we were ok. 'BUT GOD HAD A PLAN', that we didn't know about UNTIL....

Sherri began talking to her friend from back home, where we used to live 47 miles away! She tried to persuade us to come to her church, but we weren't interested. We looked back at our lives and said, We are getting nowhere, The Feeling You Get When You Don't Have God in Your Life! We didn't know it at the time. God was drawing on our hearts, and we felt ready to change our lives. So, Sherri called her friend, who explained where the church was and what time it was. We decided to go next Sunday!

CHAPTER SEVEN
Getting Saved

It was a cold and snowy Sunday, with storm warnings out, and we decided to go anyway. We had a new 4-wheel drive truck. We called Sherris' friend and said, even though the weather is bad, we are coming! If you knew me, you would never have thought I would have waited until next Sunday. Something was stirring in Sherri and me to GO! But GOD HAD A PLAN AND HE WAS WAITING ON US! So many times, we wait for God to move, but He is waiting for us to make the first move. Then, look out, because that's all it takes, most of the time, for God to move.

We loaded up and left the house at 8:00 am for the 10:00 am service. There was hardly anyone on the roads. I was surprised to see Interstate 80 had only a couple of trucks on it. We just kept telling each other, "We have to go! God was drawing on our hearts, and we didn't even realize it was Him! It was the second Sunday in February 1995! A day I will never forget the rest of my life! This was a non-denominational church, and we had no idea what kind of church that was. I was thirty-nine years old, and Sherri was thirty-eight. We had only attended a Catholic Church, as I mentioned earlier, throughout our lives. It felt like we would never get there that day. I remember saying we are too far now; we might have to stay over at our friends' for the night. I remember parts of the interstate where you could hardly see which lane you were in; that's not my driving on an interstate!

Well, we arrived about a half hour early! We went into the Church and were greeted by an older couple who lived behind me when I was growing up. The lady whom we knew from previously living in the area. She introduced me to a farmer, whom she thought I could connect with. This was all so awesome; the people greeted us and were very friendly, unlike the other churches we grew up in. We met up with Sherris' friend, with whom I was also friends, and who saved us a seat. The church had a large platform at the corner with many instruments. She told us they seat over 900 people each Sunday, one service. People were up front praying quietly, and for a tall, thin man, who our friend said was the Pastor. You feel peace in that church! The worship team came out and got ready for the service. I was starting to feel shaky inside and almost weak in my legs! I can hardly even write this right now because I'm starting to feel the same way!

Gotta take a break! Wow, I had to take a break and sit in God's Presence! As the worship team started to play, I felt as though I was taken up into Heaven and heard worship I had never heard before.

Gotta Share Something Now! If you ever feel alone, afraid, anxious, abandoned, fearful, or wanting to hurt yourself, STOP and GET ALONE and put on worship music or start thanking Jesus and don't stop until He Touches You! No one is any better than you or worse! We all struggle with life, and Jesus is there to help at every second!

As worship continued, I could hardly stand up or think about where I was; I was experiencing Total Peace being released through tears. I (Never felt that much Peace in my life! No alcohol or smoke could ever compare to God's Peace and His Presence)!!!

Before I knew it, the service ended, and I was told about the sermon. I don't remember a thing except for total peace. I went up for an altar call and surrendered my life to Jesus as my Lord and Savior. I was never taught that in my previous churches. See, salvation is available to everyone, but it's a gift —you have to take it and receive it! Just surrender and invite Jesus to forgive you, and live in you, from the heart, not just to say it! What an awesome day! Sherri came forward and invited Jesus into her life, too! I believe God had this day planned for us. See, God has a Day planned for Everyone who surrenders their life to Him. We got prayed for after receiving Jesus and walked out of the church, totally shocked and peaceful!

After Church, we headed to our friends' house for lunch and to discuss Jesus and what had happened. We stayed there until 6:00 that night for the evening service. We would go to her house every Sunday after church for nine months. What a Blessing she was, and still is!!!

I was weeping inside the whole time we were with our friends; we couldn't wait to get back to church that night! We knew something Big Had happened to us in the first service, and that we would never be the same again!

Back to the church for the second service at night. Worship started again, and the Presence of God showed up. Total peace, and the Pastor began to deliver a really good teaching. I have never heard anything like this in my life! It was so refreshing and encouraging. He read right out of the Bible and gave an illustration that was for us today. It was as if the Bible speaks directly to the people of Biblical times and to us, for what's going on in today's life. It's like you're right there experiencing it. The service lasted about an hour. The Pastor said that if anyone wanted to pray for the baptism of the Holy Spirit, they should stand in line. There were lines on the floor because it's like a gym with basketball hoops.) So, we stood in line, waiting to see what would happen; we had no idea! We felt that we could use prayer.

The Pastor got to a couple of people before me, and the person slowly fell to the ground. When he got to me, before he said anything, I hit the floor because my legs went to rubber. The power that went through my body was like nothing that ever jolted me in my life! I was pinned to the floor, and I was drunker than I ever was in my life! The peace and joy that flooded my body were beyond explanation! I don't know how long I lay there, but almost everyone had left except the Pastor, Sherri, our friend, and several others standing by me. I literally thought I was staying all night because my whole body was rubbery or paralyzed! I didn't want to move! Eventually, they brought over a chair hauler (which moved six chairs at a time), helped me up, then had me lie back on it and wheeled me out to the truck. I don't remember getting home; Sherri drove us home. I don't remember getting into bed. They told me I got baptized in the Holy Spirit. When I woke up the next morning, I was a different man. I will never forget that day, even though I don't remember the ride home or going to bed.

It was three or four days later that we both realized we had forgotten to drink wine before bed. They told me I got baptized in the Holy Spirit. (I immediately noticed many changes in me. I never talked much, but now, even today, I can't stop talking. And it's fun. I always felt unworthy of anything! Not Now, I know I'm loved by God!

Our friend asked the farmer for his phone number so I could contact him. I called him and asked him what Bible I should get, and he told me to get the New King James Spirit-Filled Life Bible! I started reading my Catholic Bible until I got my new one. I was glad I got that Bible because it was a study Bible, and that really helped me. My wife and I had some teachings years ago, and we never understood anything back then. But now I can say, when we got saved and filled with the Holy Spirit, it's a Whole New World, we can understand the Bible now!

The following week, our daughter, her boyfriend, my brother and his wife, and a friend and his wife all drove 47 miles to church. When worship started, you could feel God's Presence enter the church, and WOW, all over again! After the service, they had an altar call, and every one of them went up and got saved and filled with the Spirit! WOW! We went to our friends' house —all of us. She made lunch, and we all talked about JESUS and what was happening to us. We started meeting at our house to share Scriptures.. I talked about how I had a friend back in 1975 who came to my house and told me I had to be saved and other things. I wish I had listened to him 20 years earlier! (Gotta Share Now)! It's been about two weeks and, NO PANIC ATTACKS OR ANXIETY!!! PRAISE GOD!!!)

CHAPTER EIGHT
The New Life Begins

For the first three to twelve months after I got saved, I read the Bible between four and six hours a day, while working at the tanning business during slow times. If you are new to reading your Bible, try what an awesome brother taught me: begin in the Book of John, read **Ephesians 1:17-18**, and turn it into a prayer before you read. Holy Spirit, give me wisdom and revelation knowledge of who You are and who I am, so I can understand what You are saying to me in Jesus' Name! I did that every day for over two years! I really believe that helped me a lot, because we are asking God for help!

We displayed information and pamphlets, along with testimonies about people's lives, which sparked some good conversations at the Tanning Business. We shared our story with people in the tanning shop. People are open to listening to you share your story when you do it in love. We would ask people if they had any needs, so that we could pray for them, and most would let us pray right there.

After a couple of months, we saw several people get saved and come to our house, where we would share scriptures with them.

I shared about tithing with my brother, and he said, "Dave, I can't afford to tithe." I replied, "Read the Bible on tithing in **Malachi 3:9-11**; it clearly says we rob God if we don't." We can't afford not to tithe! In 20 years of marriage, we had struggled to make ends meet, but when we started to tithe 10% of our income before taxes, we never worried about a bill again. And you don't stop there. We are also called to give Alms and offerings above and beyond tithing! God is faithful in His promises when we obey Him!

Before too long, we had three cars making the forty-seven-mile trip to church every Sunday. We continued to go to church every Sunday and Wednesday. As I began meeting new friends, I would share my back problem with a couple of men. It was getting bad at this time! These men brought joy to me. Real men of God really care! Every week, they would ask and pray for me and my doctor, who said, "You might be in a wheelchair in a couple of years.

BUT one day, GOD put a thought in my heart, "Stop focusing and complaining, and pray for people who have back problems also! I knew it was God because it aligned with the Word. **Matthew 6:33** Seek ye the Kingdom of God and all things will be added to you! Healing is in The Kingdom of God! I needed healing! So, I prayed for people I knew who had back problems, as well as anyone I didn't know who had them.

You know this is what Jesus did! He left Heaven, where there was no sin, pain, or shame, and came to earth to destroy sin and redeem us from the curse! Jesus became the curse by hanging on the cross for ALL of us who ask! Sickness is from the curse; it's not from God! When we were born, we fell under the curse that came from Adam and Eve's sin. That's why we need a Savior, Jesus! If you don't know Him, "Now is the Time!" Ask Jesus into your Heart and Surrender Your Life to Him! I stepped out and worked one day a week in a drug and alcohol rehab, cleaning to see if I was able to work yet.

CHAPTER NINE
Moved Closer to Church

Our daughter and son–in–law were planning to get married in October. They were both living for Jesus, and my son-in-law-to-be got a job up in the oil fields about an hour away. Everything was happening so fast. We met with new believers in the area, yet we still drove 47 miles to church every Sunday and Wednesday.

We decided to put the house up for sale and see if it would sell within a couple of months, after Angie decided to get married in October. We planned to get close to the church and become more equipped for some ministry. After speaking with the Pastor, we knew we were being called into ministry. It was also the area where we grew up. We really believed it was time to make a move. We spoke with a realtor in September and decided to list the property for sale. Before we did, we prayed and asked God, if it's your will for us to move, send a buyer. The next day, it was sold!!! And we had a month to move!

Our daughter was getting married on October 14, and we had to move out by October 18, which was also our 21st wedding anniversary. WOW, our heads were spinning! At least we had already taken care of the wedding and reception plans. Now we had to say goodbye to our many friends. It was tough meeting and saying goodbye that month. So, we had to sell a lot of stuff, including our tanning business, and things we couldn't take with us! It was hard on us. It seemed like my whole life was putting down roots and then moving! This time was a joyful one, as my daughter married an awesome man of God (and still the best), moved to a great church, and grew closer to Jesus every single day with my bride.

About a year later, I kept praying and began to have less pain! I applied for a maintenance position at the church and got the job. I was on disability, and I called the Social Security Office and told them I'm going back to work, and they can take me off SSI. I began feeling better as time went by. The job taught me a lot. I learned more about humility while cleaning toilets and scrubbing floors. I even started feeling better about myself, and my back was feeling better, too. I was learning how to trust God for a complete healing and a better job!

I stepped out because the Bible said, You don't work, you don't eat, and I believed what Peter did! *God said Step out of the boat and he walked on water.* So, when we step out of our fear, God destroys the fear, and we can do anything! Just try it, that's how we gain Faith!!!

Gotta Share One More! A man in the church I met asked me if I had ever worked on cars. I told him I did and went to his house to see if I could help. He was changing a water pump on his car and couldn't get a hose back on. I tried and failed. Then I heard a thought in my heart saying, 'Why don't you ask Me?' So I asked, "Holy Spirit, help me!" Instantly, I got the problem fixed with His Help. I told him what just happened! I'm here to tell you that, even at 70 years old, every time I need help with anything, the Holy Spirit is always there to help me.

I began to realize that this Relationship with God is about an everyday relationship, whether at church, work, home, or wherever you are, the Holy Spirit is with you to help and point you to Jesus.

CHAPTER TEN
Getting Equipped

Before starting classes to get ordained, the new friend who had started the men's group and I went to Brownsville for the revival services. I never saw anything like that in my life. People were lining up outside at 3:00 AM to get into the service, which was scheduled to begin at 6:00 PM that evening. They had good worship every night, and the evangelist spoke for about an hour. Then a young girl sang "Come To the Mercy Seat". I would say at least 100-500 people ran to the Altar every night to get saved! The Pastor stepped off the stage and fell on me. I immediately began praying with great urgency, and it still comes over me at times today. My friend and I were able to stay for the entire week at a pastor's conference. When I stepped into that church every night, I began to weep, and it felt good. I was told that God's presence was so strong that our bodies couldn't handle it. I didn't want to leave that place ever! When we got home, I knew it was time to step out and begin taking classes to get ordained for ministry!

I acknowledged that I had a call to ministry in my life, and even though I was 42 years old, I wanted more of God and to share God's love with people. While taking classes for ministry, I resigned from my church job and began working in a Career Center as an Aide. I really loved this job because I had a heart for kids, especially those who were challenged. My job was to work four days a week with the students. Carpentry shop two days a week, and Building construction two days a week. The carpentry shop was primarily focused on home building, while the Building Trades shop performed various tasks, including carpentry, block laying, electrical work, plumbing, and maintenance. I got along well with the students, and it gave me a real sense of accomplishment. I enjoyed helping the students see their potential, which they never knew they had.

I found out that the more you encourage them, the better they become at what they're learning. It was a joy to see the excitement on their faces when they completed their project. When you encourage a student, he can trust you and even open up to you. That was the goal: to gain their trust and share the Love of Jesus with them. I had several opportunities to interact with the students and teachers during my time there.

 When I got the job, the Director told me I would probably be sick, off and on, until I built up my immunity, because there is always someone sick in the class. I said to myself, That's not going to happen! I was the guy who always said, "I'll be sick next, when I was around sick people! I prayed to myself every time I was around a sick student, and I never got sick that whole school year!

That really showed me how powerful Scripture is because I prayed Scripture every time! I also learned about how society has changed since I was in school. I also took Carpentry in a 'Career Center'. In Grades ten through twelve, we wanted to work in the shop; it was an honor to be allowed in back then. Some students today, not all, seem to lack motivation to work. That was part of our job, to make it interesting to them! That was a real challenge because I told them it wouldn't be that way when they graduate and get a job! I told them the truth so they would be equipped for the real world.

That is a priority with The Lord, putting others ahead of yourself and demonstrating Godly principles every day. We are called to demonstrate Jesus while we are here on earth. When you're doing God's will, it's not work, it's pleasure!!! *The key is to step out of your boat and start doing what God puts in your heart, not your friends' hearts.* You will be totally excited to see what God has for you! Remember what He calls you to; He will equip you when you step out —usually not before! I know He showed me ways to get the students excited about what they're learning and how well they are progressing!

At the same time, God was working in me to reach out to people who might not have a good life; I can relate, but God can change your heart and your focus! See, His Word talks a lot about what we think and say. Our words are important, and our thoughts will direct our actions! The book of James, chapter three, has a great deal to say. Check it out! We are always in training, so don't give up! The closer I get to God, the more I'm trying to watch my words!

While still taking classes, I also reached out to a couple of jails to volunteer for Bible studies. Another valuable lesson: you don't have to know everything, but when you step out, you will learn very quickly! The Holy Spirit is waiting for us to step out, because He will empower us and speak through us. This is a great way to gain Faith! Also, it glorifies God when you share what He does in your life! This is all training grounds, I keep saying, because it's true! God's not looking for perfect people, just those who are available to do His will. The memories will last a Lifetime!!! Step out of your boat!!! That's all it takes! Trust Him! He will never let you down!

CHAPTER ELEVEN
Stepped Out Into Construction

I completed the ministry schooling and became an ordained Minister! I decided to return to construction work while waiting for a Ministry job. My Pastor prayed for me to move out into a new field. And when I stepped out of the boat, the jobs were there, one right after another!

I hired a fifteen-year-old Amish boy who worked like an eighteen-year-old. We began doing small remodeling jobs. He worked for me for about a year. He was just about the hardest-working man I ever met. When I taught him something new, he remembered how to do the job from then on. He was also extremely smart at figuring out a job and doing math. They go to 8th grade, but he could keep up with high school kids in math and in the quality of his work.

When he moved on to another contractor, we remained friends for a long time. He moved on because I hired his Father, and they decided that he should step down. They have different ways. I respected their decision, and it worked out well. Shortly after hiring the Amish Dad, we became very busy and expanded our business, and I bought a work van. We were working on roofs, hanging and finishing drywall. During this expansion, I felt like I was getting healed by at least 90%. I wasn't in business to hire men to do all the work. I worked full-time and kept up with the workers.

A tragedy happened to the Amish workers' sister's family with a tragic house fire. The entire community came together and built a new house, including the basement, in just three days! We went back a month later and had to cut the bottoms of every door at an angle because the house had settled. However, this was necessary because the family had an urgent need for a place to live. It was a tragedy, but a blessing to see everyone available who offered their support and help from the community.

We began to receive more opportunities to expand our services. We got into home remodeling, windows, doors, flooring, roofing, siding, small additions, and garages. I hired my nephew, who turned out to be a great asset. Even the Amish man said, 'I can't believe how quickly he picks it up on the projects we do.' He said you show him once, and he got it.

My nephew was even laying out additions and estimating material. I approached him after a year and asked if he wanted to be a partner in the business. He said he was going to go to college because he had seen how hard it was on the body and didn't want to go down that path. He worked with us for a couple of years. What a Blessing he was!

Gotta Tell This Story! The Amish man and I always listened to worship music and Christian teachings on the job and in the van. He would sing and agree with whoever was teaching that day. One day, on the way home to drop him off, we worshiped some good worship songs, and you could feel the Presence of the Lord in the van. When we arrived at his buggy, he opened the door and fell out laughing. He said, "What is that feeling? I said, that is the Presence of God!!! He said, "That is awesome! Oh, I could tell a hundred stories about the presence of God in the 14 years we worked together!

One day, we were remodeling a bathroom for a friend I used to work with at the Career Center. She asked me if I would be interested in teaching students about Building Construction. I told her I would, and she said to have a resume ready and bring it to school by 8:00 A.M. tomorrow. I had to scramble to figure out how to fill out a resume and get it typed that night. The next day, I made it on time and went back to work that afternoon. I had to explain to the Amish man that I might be leaving in three months to teach school. We continued working and having a good time together. We worked hard every day, but we also had a great friendship and a great time on the job. We had his family over on Christmas every year and got together often. Those were the days I will always remember, and I still see him every Amish Benefit Auction on the first Saturday of June!

Thank You, Lord, for the opportunity and experience you blessed me with working for an awesome man! During those 14 years, we had another Amish man who helped us build a barn and other projects. Once you get to know the Amish and if they like you, you have made many good friends. I learned a lot from the Amish. They take care of each other very well, and all come together when needed, from building a barn to building a house.

CHAPTER TWELVE
Teaching Job at Career Center

I had an interview with the director and principal of the Career Center, where I was required to give a demonstration of teaching a class. I chose how to lay out and square a building. The interview went well, and they called a week later to schedule a follow-up interview. I was hired and was told I would have to apply and take college classes. The classes were focused on (How to Teach). It was set up to take four years for one degree and six more for a complete degree. So, it took ten years to complete. I took the first four years and stopped there. With that degree, I could teach for twelve years. I was 64 years old at that time.

So, now I go from swinging a hammer to spending many hours on a computer every day. I desperately needed help. A couple of teachers would come every day and help me learn the computer. God will equip the called, so don't think you have to know everything. He puts people in your path to get you to where you need to be!

We had in-service days and time to prepare the classroom and shop for the incoming students. I started preparing a month early. I was to teach Building Construction, which included carpentry, masonry, electricity, plumbing, and HVAC, to tenth to twelfth grade students. I had half the county schools in the morning for 3.5 hours, and the other half in the afternoon for the same amount of time. I had 10th graders through 12th graders together in both sessions. That wasn't easy at first.

College classes, at first, taught us how to prepare a comprehensive safety program for all power and hand tools to be used in the shop. We had to create our own handouts and hands-on demonstrations for the students to complete, along with a test to get signed off on using that specific tool. Students were not allowed into the shop unless they passed the shop safety rules. It took the students a week to complete the shop safety rules.

On the first day of school, I received a call at home about my brother. He had been rushed to the hospital, and I was given no more details. I called my sister-in law, who told me he was in the ICU on a kidney machine. I went right up to the hospital, and the doctor was in his room and said, his kidneys shut down, and that's all they know. What a tough time to go through.

I went up every day after school. The third day, they took him off the machine, and I was there. The doctor said, "We are going to find out why they shut down." I felt so bad for him, and I was struggling with the school job. I wanted to quit the job and go back into business.

At the same time, my heart was breaking for my brother. We got a call that evening from my sister-in-law that it was the medication he was on that caused his kidneys to shut down. About 3:00 A.M., we got another call to go to the hospital, because something was wrong with my brother. We got there right away, and they said he developed a massive blood clot in his lungs from the kidney machine, and they gave him two different blood thinners. My brother was lying there singing worship songs to God, but was unconscious to any of us! I saw the doctor come in, run to the monitors, and an image of a head appeared. The doctor put both hands on his head and said, NO, NO! The doctor came over to us and said, "He has no brain function, his brain hemorrhaged from the blood thinners he is passing as we speak!" What a SAD situation. He was lying there worshipping God as he passed!!! I had to go to school that day, and it was extremely hard! That made my first semester the most challenging thing I've ever had to do in my life! Thank You, Jesus, for Your Peace in the storms of life. It was hard, but he walked through them with you every step.

Gotta tell a story! The first day of school came, and what a surprise: I thought the students would be excited to take a three-year course in building construction. We were required to wear a suit to class. When I got home, my wife asked, 'What in the world happened to you?' I guess I looked bad. The students were out of control, and everything I did made it worse. The students came in with an attitude that they were going to run the class.

I spent a month in the office with the principal during my lunch break every day. I didn't realize you can't discipline them! It wasn't like it was when I went to school. It was a privilege to attend a Career Center when I went to school! I took carpentry and made a career out of it! I learned very quickly that part of the job was teaching the students to want to be there! This was all new to me. Kids seem to play a big role in running schools today. I did have some awesome co-workers who helped me learn the ropes.

Building lesson plans and job handouts became easier with co-workers' help. The problem was teaching three grades simultaneously. We had projects running at the same time, which kept the shop always full.

First-year students worked on hand tool projects after completing all safety tests. Second-year students began laying out small projects across all trades and completing them according to diagrams in the handouts. All students had to take a refresher course and pass with 100% on safety. The Senior class began practicing layout for their tiny house project. The class practiced laying blocks, then they laid their foundation blocks and began building. The morning class would complete a kitchen, and the afternoon class would complete a bathroom. In the middle of the building, each class built 4x4 rooms with a toilet and sink. The building was complete with electrical plumbing, tile floors, drywall finished and painted. The exterior was vinyl-sided, with brick halfway up the front. Students also wired a complete 100-amp service panel and service entrance wire to the pole and installed a weatherhead.

The seniors completed a very challenging state test at the end of the year. It wasn't required to pass, but it was their last nine-week grade. Students did very well.

Back to the college class I had to take. The professor came to the school and graded me on how well I taught the class according to the lesson plan. Our lesson plans were 3.5 pages long. The professor also graded us on how we handled students who weren't paying attention to the teaching. You also had those students who tried to stir the pot.

It was hard to teach and go to college at the same time at 52 years old. I would ask the Holy Spirit for help. I would wake up many nights with the answer to what to do next in the shop, and for the college classes and tests. If it wasn't for the Holy Spirit, I can honestly say, I would not have made it as a teacher. He was at my side every day without a doubt. "The Bible says, I will never leave you nor forsake you"!

The job was extremely challenging every day, but it kept me on my toes. If your bad student had not been there that day, another student would have stepped in to stir the pot. It made for interesting days, but it was very rewarding for those who wanted to be there. I found out the disruptive students just needed more attention. So, we would handle each situation by making them feel important; it worked almost every time. I always tried to make the students feel like we were one team. No one is better than another, as far as being a part of the team.

*Gotta Share a Story....*I would always create an opportunity to share Jesus in the shop. One year, I had a student who got a text from his Mom asking for prayer for their neighbor's boy, who had fallen down the steps. Every student held hands, and we prayed for the little boy. About two hours later, his Mom called and said, "The little boy was okay and thanked us for praying. The students were so excited, and they really felt like they were part of the little boy being ok. Those are situations that those kids will never forget.

I had a little person in my class for three years. He came into the classroom the first day of school in silky gym shorts, dragging them along the ground, and a backpack three layers deep. He could hardly walk; it was so heavy. He was always getting in trouble. He was a strong young man.

In the shop, we had lockers for students to change clothes. Each student had to purchase a lock from the school and keep their locker locked at all times. The students had four minutes to change clothes, shoes, and leave for the bus. So, there was always confusion and sometimes a little arguing, and I told them they were young adults and needed to handle this situation as maturing students. One day, two students came to me and said, "They can't unlock their lockers! So, I had a key and unlocked them. Next morning, the same problem! So, we had a meeting and, as usual, no one knew anything about the problem! I watched the students get in their lockers at the end of the period, and I noticed my little man was at eye level with the locks! I told him I was going to keep an eye on him and maybe both eyes on him. I noticed he was a pro at pulling jokes, and it would be hard to catch him in the act. I told him some other students saw him switching locks during shop time. He just smiled and said he would never do that.

We used to have a break in each class. The principal caught him banging on another shop's window. That was the end of the breaks for a while. One more story! At the end of the period, one student couldn't find one of his shoes. I looked at my little man's face, and he looked up in the rafters, where it was, and I said, If you don't have that shoe back here in one minute, you're going to the office. He was a strong guy! He ran up the ladder to the project's roof, jumped up, grabbed the metal trusses, pulled himself onto the roof, and came back down in time. When he left that day, I laughed so hard and told the other teachers at lunchtime, and they laughed too. One more story, he could run down the hall and slide on his stomach on the floor with his hands and feet in the air.

I told the students that I went to prison on Thursday night to do a Bible study. They were really impressed. Every Thursday, they would ask if I was going to prison that night! Then, on Friday, they would ask what happened. That went on for many years. I told them the downfalls of breaking the law and the freedom they lose. I told them about the inmates who invited Jesus into their lives, and the change they were demonstrating. They wanted to talk the whole period if I let them. I had each class for 3.25 hours.

A couple of us teachers started prayer time in the morning before we had to report to the classroom. We saw that our situation had changed through prayer. I really miss those times. We have to encourage each other. After a while, we all said we needed this time of encouragement. God is so Good, He shows up every time you welcome Him!

I had teachers who wouldn't come to prayer time, but when they had trouble, they came to me for questions and prayer. Not one of those teachers ever laughed or made fun of me. They were the greatest men and women to work with. We all had each other's backs! A couple of teachers sent students who struggled with life to talk to me. I believe God is so needed in the schools. They took Him out years ago, but He never left! If you're reading this, don't stop praying or giving up, God is always there to help you and the students!!!

At the beginning of every school year, I asked the Lord what He wanted to teach me that year, and the Lord would put a thought in my heart! I'll share the last two years with you…. That thought my second-to-last year was 'Love the unlovable extra this year!' There were a lot of them in this world. I felt it was mostly at school, but also out of school. At this time, I was also going into prison every week doing a Bible study, which I'll share in another chapter.

When I focused on the unlovable, I began to see more than I thought I would. They were everywhere, and I began to show them grace when I didn't think they deserved it. I began to realize I didn't deserve it from God either. It drastically changed my heart when I saw how guilty we all are about being unlovable at times, and God still graces us. Wow, what an eye-opener! God is so good at lovingly revealing our faults. He puts a situation in our path, and we begin to see ourselves in it as well. Thank You, Lord, for helping me see my faults and appreciate Your grace. Now I see why we are to grace others.

God gives us Grace even when we don't deserve it. Grace is unmerited favor. **Ephesians 2:8** says: *we are saved by grace, not our own doing, but a gift from God, not a result of works, so that no one may boast!* That's awesome news. So, if you're reading this and have never asked Jesus into your life, this is what God does for you because he sent His Son, Jesus, to the Cross to pay the price for your sins! It's His Gift of Grace, freedom not deserved. So, that is who we are to become, givers of Grace to others!

In my final year of teaching, I felt the Lord had given me a challenge I thought would be easy. He put it in my heart too: (Love the lovable and expect nothing in return). I thought it would be easy because I really like people! Little did I know I had to learn a big lesson this time.

I began to realize that some people whom I loved weren't returning any love at all! This probably happened many times before, but I wasn't aware of it happening until the spotlight was on them now. Wow, God knows how to open our eyes by putting situations in our lives and exposing our real hearts. Many people at this time will think people are picking on them, or that they are not real friends. I want to say that most of the time God is showing us what He wants to set us free from, but we miss it. Our hearts should always see each situation as a lesson God wants us to learn, not as an excuse to justify our actions. See, we exchanged our rights for His when we surrender our lives to Him. No longer are my ways right, but God's ways are what's right. His ways always bring freedom and peace!

So, for that school year, I was learning about loving others and not expecting love in return. See, God wants us not to be people pleasers but to be people who God loves unconditionally and wants us to realize His Love Is Sufficient!!! When we want it from others, we can never please God. Don't get me wrong —we still love people unconditionally, but if we don't get it in return, that's okay! We get it from God! That's what's called a relationship with God. Not Religion!

The overall school experience taught me many lifelong lessons on how to live a Christian life in tough situations. I met so many good co-workers and keep in touch with them. I learned so much about why this younger generation sees life differently from my generation. I feel bad for them because they miss a lot of important things about growing up and having fun. We were outside all the time until dark, playing some ball game, while they sat in front of a computer game about hurting each other. I'm afraid this is not good for their well-being. My prayer is that this will change, and the next generation will not harm their brains by sitting in front of a computer playing unhealthy games all day; they can get outside and enjoy life again. The statistics are staggering about the harm these video games do to our precious young generation. Mom and Dads, you have your work cut out for you. These children are precious, every one of them. Remember God gave them to you as precious gifts! Blessings to You! Thank You, Lord, for allowing me to spend time and influence these precious children of Yours!!

CHAPTER THIRTEEN
First Mission Trip to Saltillo, Mexico

About two years after we got saved, Sherri and I went on our first out-of-the-country mission trip to Saltillo, Mexico. We practiced what we were going to do and prepared to go out of the country, taking malaria pills and shots, as well as skits we were going to perform in the streets. We were pumped and ready to visit Mexico! There were about eight of us from the church, along with an interpreter from another church. We flew to Texas, then to Monterey, Mexico, and finally took a bus to Saltillo. Wow, what a poor town. We have never seen anything like this in our lives. We all stayed in a nice house.

We went to a church service that night, and a little girl, about eight to ten years old, came and asked the leader of our group, who was from there, if we could come to her house because her mother was dying of cancer. Sherri and I, along with our pastor and the host group leader, walked over to the house of the sick woman.

On our way over, it looked like a war zone, with homes made of crates, cardboard, and cement blocks, and no doors, windows, or floors. We were devastated. All you want to do is cry! We went into the house, and on one mattress lay an old lady who was about 90 pounds, and on the other mattress was Mom. Both mattresses were on top of four cement blocks, one at each corner. Mom weighed about 80 pounds. Dirt floor, no windows in the openings, no door in the door opening. Nothing else in the house. Five kids and no Dad that we know of.

Oh my, anyone who saw that would be devastated! I had to step out for a minute to cry my eyes out. There was a pie pan on each bed with pink stuff in it to kill the flies. It was covered with flies. We prayed for Mom and asked if there was anything we could do to help. The little kids held my hand and wouldn't let go! We all cried our eyes out on the walk back to the church. These homes were all in a desert, right out in the sun. The average high temperature while we were there was over 100 degrees. No humidity, though, and it's cold at night. This was the beginning of what we would see on our trip. It was a major eye-opener on how many people must live. You wouldn't believe it if you didn't see it. It still bothers me when I think about it because those people will live like that for the rest of their lives.

At night, we went to the town park and put on skits to share the Gospel. We told the people that satan is a liar and he is the one who causes fear and anxiety. He puts bad thoughts in your head and lies about everything.

Then we told them about the God who created them and that He sent His only Son, Jesus, to come to earth through a virgin woman named Mary. That is why people all over the world celebrate Christmas. We tell them about how Jesus was baptized in a river, that the Holy Spirit came on Him, and that He healed and delivered people, and that His purpose was to come to earth and sacrifice His life on a cross to pay the full price for our sins. His presence is here right now because He lives with those who believe in Him. He wants everyone to come to Him and surrender their lives to Him by asking Jesus into their heart and repenting of their sins. He will give them a new heart and put the Holy Spirit in them. When we surrender to Him, He will open the door to the Father for us. The Father will look at us then as His children forever.

That night, we had a large outcome, and several people came forward and gave their lives to Jesus. They allowed us to pray for them and show them God's love. There was a local Pastor with us who helped them get connected to a church, because if you don't get connected, you won't really know God. Almost everyone who doesn't get connected falls away because you won't understand what it means to develop a relationship with God. God has a plan and purpose for each one of us, and it includes being with believers. It is a major part of developing that relationship and becoming disciples. Church leaders have effective programs to help disciple new believers.

We continued to go to the park every night and reach out to whoever was there. We would have a large crowd every night. The people would go to the park at night for something to do. People came to watch the skit we performed every night, then stayed to listen to the local pastor explain salvation and the relationship with Jesus. Each night was a powerful experience, unlike anything I had seen in America. People were hungry for truth and Jesus. They have a simple life, free of worry about their stuff.

These people were more family-oriented and led simple lives. At night, everyone is out late, sitting in chairs, socializing with their neighbors, laughing, and having good, clean fun. I wish we had that here in America. Here we come home from work, push a button to open our garage door, pull the car in, shut the door, and hardly ever talk to our neighbor. I heard people say, "We don't even know our neighbors." I think Jesus has more for us than that. As I watched the people in Saltillo, Mexico, they don't have much of anything, but they are richer than we are here in America! They have joy and true love for each other. Lord, move in the hearts of Americans to let go of our expensive stuff and get back to the basics of loving God, life, and our neighbor!

Thank You, Lord, for allowing me to be a blessing to the people of Mexico and for the new love for my brothers and sisters that I got to share on my first mission trip out of the country.

CHAPTER FOURTEEN
Mission Trip Two - Another trip to Saltillo

On this trip, I was asked by the mission Pastor at the church I attend. It was about two plus years later. We prepared to perform skits again to reveal Satan's schemes and what Jesus did to set us free from our sins, fear, shame, and deliverance from all evil forces! This trip will be a little different because I remember the last trip and what I experienced, but you can never feel that way because we have no idea what God wants us to do. We need to be open to His plan, even though we have a plan of our own!

We landed in Monterey, Mexico, and waited for the van to arrive for our two to three-hour trip to Saltillo. You can't get impatient there; nothing moves fast. I think God was teaching me patience! I always heard from others, Don't ask for patience!

The Van arrived, and we reached our base by late afternoon. We unloaded and were told we have a special Pastor who was going to be with us this week, who we will really appreciate, on this week of ministering to the lost.

We will call him Pastor Jaun. Pastor Juan ministered to the lost, sick, and anyone who needed help up in the mountains. Up in the mountains lived native Mexican people. The only doctors up there are those whom the tribespeople call "Witch Doctors." This is why Pastor Juan goes up there because the Lord ordained him to go to that area. We all have a calling in our lives! Do you know yours?

Pastor Juan shared many stories with us that week. I will never forget the story he told us: how the witch doctors had no power to bring healing or freedom to anyone, but Pastor Juan had God's power. He went to a place of their worship, and there were a couple of people wrapped in their burial clothing for a day or two. Pastor Juan prayed over them, and God raised them from the dead! Wow, to hear him tell the story was awesome! You could feel the power of God when he told the story. It is a different world in Mexico. My eyes were beginning to open to how much stuff we have in America that we don't need!

We spent one morning listening to a good message by the Pastor on what Jesus did the afternoon before Good Friday. The disciples and Jesus shared a meal called the Last Supper. When they finished supper, Jesus got up and prepared what He would teach the disciples —the final and most important teaching.

Jesus poured a basin of water and began to wash the disciples' feet one by one. Jesus was demonstrating the most humble and powerful example to His disciples before going to the Cross. This was an example He was demonstrating to them of how to live your life with humility and love. This was also for them to share with the world that Jesus came to humble Himself and to take all the sins of the world to the Cross, paying the price in full!

That morning, the Pastor began washing our feet, and we washed each other's feet in turn. There wasn't a dry eye all morning in that room. You could feel God's Presence all morning! Today, when I think about that morning, I feel humbled, peace, and love from God. I believe we can never get close enough to God, but the closer we get, the more peace we will have in our lives, and do what He commands: love each other more. When we weep because of what God does in us, it really brings a deep cleansing.

We went back out into the park and performed our skits, and the Pastor shared the love of Jesus with the crowd. Many people came that night and surrendered their lives to Jesus. Every night, the crowd grew bigger, and more people wanted prayer and just to be loved on. Many people are looking for truth and hope; Jesus is the answer. When you see them surrender their lives, it really touches your heart! It's real, Jesus is Real! We had a little girl, about 16, who served as my interpreter as we shared every night after the skit. She was so precious. When someone got saved, tears would run down her cheeks. My prayer is that every new believer experiences this transformation. They will never be the same again!

Getting ready to finish the week out, and Pastor Juan asked if we wanted to be baptized in the small pool they had at the base! We all said, YES! So, the next day, we all got ready to be baptized by Pastor Juan.

As each person was baptized in water, Pastor Juan shared what he felt God was saying to them. This is called 'prophecy.' Pastor Juan lived his whole life on hearing from God where to go and what his assignment was! He was probably in his mid-sixties. What a Man of God! He would speak in Spanish, and our interpreter would tape what he said and translate it into English as he spoke.

When he came to me, he started crying. He baptized me and began to prophesize, saying; God has placed angels over me and given me grace to win hundreds and thousands to the Lord! He said much more, but I don't want to point to myself because anything I accomplish in this world is because of God's Grace and provision! None of us is worthy, but because we are His ambassadors, He empowers us to do what we can't do to reach the lost! We completed our trip that day with a big blessing and returned home the next day. It was sad to leave Pastor Juan, knowing we probably won't see him again until we meet in Heaven! Thank You, Lord, for the awesome experience of being in Your Presence and seeing all that You have done in Mexico!

CHAPTER FIFTEEN
Third Mission Trip - Last Trip to Mexico

This trip came by being asked again to go to Mexico with our Church missions Pastor to meet with Pastors from five different Counties. The goal was to help unite Pastors in Mexico. We met many other Pastors who were already united together. On our first Sunday in Mexico, we attended a church, and a lady came up to me, very excited, and started talking to me in Spanish. Our interpreter met her and started translating what she was saying into English.

The interpreter said she had seen my face in her dreams and visions for many months. She said, I will come to Mexico and bring peace and unity to our country. I was floored and didn't know what to say. I told the interpreter to tell her I don't understand what she means. She was persistent and kept saying that I saw your face many times. Our Pastor shared this with the other Pastors and asked them to pray about what it means and to share with them what I am to do, if anything. I prayed and asked God what I was supposed to do. I was excited, but I asked God to show me.

We continued meeting with other Pastors who were coming together to pray for God's will for unity in Mexico. We traveled a lot and met Pastors from five different counties, all of whom were excited to come together. One thing I noticed about people from Mexico is that they don't have much, but their relationship with God is greater to them than anything this world has to offer. I believe they can teach us a lot about what it means to be a Christian in a fallen world.

I saw many churches with statues inside, and people came in, put money in a box in front of the statue, and prayed. None of the Pastors we met did any of that. Their church service was just like ours here in America. They really worshipped God with all their heart! Their messages were very uplifting and pointed to how to live your life for God. They have a love for each other that we don't have in America. They are very poor and very happy. I think their hope and trust are in God, but we mix our hope in God with material things and our careers.

The trip ended very well. Our missions Pastor met many Pastors over the years before she felt God wanted her to help unite them. It was a Blessing for me to meet and be a part of this Ministry.

In conclusion, my wife and I discussed the woman at the church who had a vision and our next step. So, went to our head Pastor for his thoughts. He said we should pray for a while, and he will also. He also said, meet with our interpreter and pray about going and spending some time learning Spanish. The Mexican Pastors thought they might be able to come and Pastor a church after learning the language and becoming better equipped. We had a lot to pray about. We did start meeting with an interpreter and taking Spanish lessons. Some of the elders thought we were too young as Christians to step out this early in our walk with God. We agreed it was too early and that, after several months, we should pass on this opportunity. Thank You, Lord, for all the experience and opportunities You blessed us with!

CHAPTER SIXTEEN
Fourth Mission Trip - Off To Venezuela

I had the opportunity to go on a mission trip to Venezuela with Mission Aviation Fellowship! Nickname MAF. We flew for five hours to Caracas. Then we took a smaller plane, 2.5 hours to Port Ayacucho. We got off the plane, and all we saw were armed guards. We then took a bus to the MAF Base. We went there to help work on the base MAF.

We spent about four to six days installing tongue-and-groove boards on all the ceilings. We worked eight to ten hours a day, cutting and installing all the boards. We enjoyed our conversations with the pilots. We got close to a pilot who was a Native American from the western United States.

Towards the end of our trip, the American pilot took three of us on a 90-minute flight to a village in the jungles of Venezuela. The plane was a four-seater aircraft with landing gear designed for grassy runways. So, we loaded into the airplane one morning very early and headed to the jungle. On our trip, we saw what volcanoes looked like for most of our trip. It was my first time flying in a little plane, and it was shaking and loud. I must admit, I was a little scared because we hit turbulence on and off most of the way.

We landed on a grassy runway and stopped about six feet from the wooded area at the edge of the jungle. I don't know how the pilots do this because we bounced the whole time when we hit the ground, and you couldn't even focus on anything looking out the window. On top of all that, there were three fuselages at the beginning of the landing strip, and the pilot said the planes wrecked there while coming in for a landing. We landed, turned around, and rode up about five feet, and there were about 20-25 kids, no clothes on, with stomachs that stuck out, ready to burst. I sat in that plane and cried for about ten minutes because I had a vision of what I was looking at, when I was about ten to twelve years old, in a Catholic church, listening to a missionary talk about her work in South America. It was totally unbelievable to me!!!

We got out of the plane, and the kids swarmed us! We had a warm welcome from the Pastor and Leader of the tribe, who happened to be the same man. He was wearing gym shorts just like we did in high school, the same color. He also had a pair of winter see-through plastic boots, and that was all.

There is a missionary couple who have been there for many years, and they communicate with the MAF pilot using a generator and a Ham Radio. They weren't there at the time. The wife is still working there but has taken a leave because her husband died.

We were shown around the village and ate this white, flat bread that looked like a pizza shell, which they pulled off the bamboo roof. It's made from cassava, which they call yuca. They told us it had almost no nutritional value. I wondered all day if we'd get sick from eating it. We'd forgotten to bring extra bottles of water, so we had only one to share under the brutal, humid heat.

Across the Amazon River, we could hear the deep wailing of mourners for a man who'd died the night before of alcohol poisoning. Another group from the tribe was out hunting monkeys, their main source of meat. A small boy, maybe four or five, clung to my hand as we walked. The people lived in thatched huts, smoky inside to drive away insects and preserve the roofs. Each hut held only hammocks—no beds or furniture—because of snakes and other creatures that wandered at night.

The pastor showed us the dugout canoes they carved from logs. Then we saw women using a long, vine-woven press to squeeze the poisonous juice from grated cassava pulp. After pressing, they baked the dry fibers into the thin cassava bread we had eaten. It was exactly like scenes from National Geographic—women barely clothed, children with round bellies from malnutrition, and a simplicity that was both raw and unforgettable.

The Pastor wanted to take us on a walk through the jungle to see the new project they just started. The project was clearing a small area and planting peppers and other vegetables. We walked across a long log that was over the Amazon River and saw leaves as big as I was. Yes, the little boy still had my hand! We got to see their garden, the fruit trees they were growing, and the beautiful forests.

When we returned to the tribe, we took a break and discussed plans to build a church the following year. The tribe was going to cut down and prepare the trees and prepare the location for the church; the pilot was going to bring out metal roofing a little at a time in his plane. Their church was going to be like a pavilion.

The tribe makes wooden bowls and spoons, blowguns, and arrows to sell at the market near the MAF base. The pilot takes everything to the market, and what they make from their products, the pilot brings back in soap and salt. That's all they purchase for outside the jungle.

I purchased a blowgun and a quiver with ten arrows as a souvenir to take home. That afternoon, we said goodbye, and the pilot took one guy who came with us and a missionary who was going home. He took a 10-minute flight, dropped us off on another grassy runway, and returned to pick up my Pastor and me because the plane only held five of us.

Before they arrived, we were sitting with the kids waiting for the pilot to return. We gave the kids each a piece of gum, and they did not know what to do with it. Not a good idea, they had it everywhere. While we were sitting there, the little boy still had my hand (six plus hours), and the other kids must never see hair on anyone's arms because they tried to pull mine off.

While we were there, a man still had his face painted from the party the night before came and sat between me and the blow gun. The man kept staring at the gun and me back and forth. I was getting nervous. The plane landed and turned around, and we stood up to go. I grabbed the blowgun and arrows and walked to the plane with my shoulders back, anticipating his spear coming toward me. Thank God it didn't happen! I figured he might be dangerous, carrying a spear when no one else was.

We left and ran into a storm on our way back to the base. I had a very interesting trip, I'll never forget. I'm extremely Thankful that God let me have this experience, especially the vision I had 35-40 years earlier, which came true when I least expected it! When I think about this trip, I would never have believed these people still live like this. Thank You, Lord, and I pray I could be a vessel You will use to share Your love with many of Your people!!!

CHAPTER SEVENTEEN
Prison Ministry

About two years after I surrendered my life to Jesus, I felt led to share my faith and God's Word in a prison. I applied at a local jail that housed local offenders and state inmates. I had to get clearances, meet the warden, learn the rules, and get a quick orientation. They asked if I wanted to minister to both men and women.

I said, men only. I received all my clearances, photo badge, and time/day set. I could start going in. I'm allowed in at 6:00 pm every Thursday for two blocks. Each block contained 67 guys, and they are always full.

My first day came, and I had a friend promise to call me at 5:50 pm every day I go in. On my way in, the powers of darkness reminded me of my fear and anxiety, and I said, No Way, I'm set free by the Blood of Jesus Christ! I entered the prison and was escorted upstairs, passing through seven locked doors and two elevator doors, none of which I could control.

After going through the first door, I was flooded with the Peace of God, and that happened every time I went in for over 16-18 years. I knew I was in the right place. When we get a strong thought to step out of our boat to minister to someone, step out, and if peace comes, you're in the right place! You will know right away! But if we don't step out, we may be missing what God wants for us!

I was met by another guard, who announced that anyone who wanted to attend Bible study should enter the designated room. I can't remember how many came in, but the whole block just stood there and looked at me. I instantly felt God's power come over me, and a feeling that He is there in a powerful way. He also began to break my heart for these guys and removed thoughts.

I entered the small room, about 12 x 12 feet. I introduced myself, and they did likewise. I opened in prayer and began to share, really quickly, my story and a small teaching I had prepared. The inmates were very interested and treated me with great respect. This really humbled me. These guys responded with thankfulness I never expected. I was excited, and before I knew it, two hours had gone by, and I got to go across the hall to another block. The same thing happened there.

Everyone stared at me again. Another group of men came into the study. Time went by very fast again, and at 9:40 pm, the guard spoke to us over a speaker, and the door unlocked. The guard said, You have 15 minutes to be in your cells. They escorted me downstairs to the exit.

Wow, I couldn't wait to get home and tell my wife! She was excited for me. I tried to encourage her to sign up for the women's block, but she wasn't interested. I thanked the men's group I was involved with. I shared all that went on in the prison and how many doors I had to go through, and I had no control over them.

I have so many stories to share, like one day I was just going into the first block and there were two inmates in the room fighting because one told the other one he wasn't taking it seriously enough. I never thought I would experience that. Another time, I just got up on the block, and a fight broke out. The guards were quick to respond. One guard must have been assigned to me. He grabbed me and pulled me into the 10x10 room between the inside and outside doors. Those guys were all built; some of them had no neck from all the muscles. That surprised me by the speed and the split second it took to defuse the problem, with no one hurt.

Another story I could share is about a man with an abscessed tooth who couldn't read well. We all prayed for him to be healed of his toothache and be able to read. The next week I went back, and his jaw was back to normal. He said that, with help from another inmate, he was starting to read a lot better and understand what he was reading.

After about ten years, they decided to change our schedule. There was always an older Catholic man, with whom I would trade blocks after two hours. They decided we would pick one block each, and hours would change to 6:00 pm to 9:00 pm. I preferred to be in both blocks and shorten the time.

I called the Warden for permission to bring in a small CD player, leave it with the front guard, and pick it up before going on the block. That way, they knew there was no contraband in it. He permitted me. In the first week, the guard said he didn't have permission to give it to me. I called the Warden, and he said he would take care of it. For the next 12 weeks, because I kept a log, the C.O. on the block told me he didn't care what the warden said, I wasn't getting the CD player. So that ended that. I gave up after thirteen weeks. I was just thankful I was able to take the Gospel to the inmates.

I told all my friends that what really surprised me was that the Holy Spirit is in prisons. I would feel God's power in there sometimes more than in the church services, even though our church services were powerful. When I think about it, I went from a church where nobody would talk to each other to one where everyone seemed to talk to each other. Don't say that as criticism, but it's sad it's that way.

Another story in the one block I went to know: there was a guy in there who looked tough —shaved head, tattoos everywhere, looking like he should be playing pro football. Out of my mouth came, "Brother, tonight God wants to break the chains of witchcraft and anger in your life." He said, "How did you know?" I said, "I don't know; God knows." And if you want to be free, now is the time! I asked if anyone here has doubts about God's ability to set him free. Please step out of the room now. No one moved. I asked everyone to agree in prayer, and they did. We prayed, and he began to sweat profusely and said, "I'm free. What an Awesome God we serve!!! What an amazing deliverance those inmates witnessed, boosting their faith in what our "God Can Do!"

One of the things I really struggled with was that, for the eight to ten years I worked construction, I was beat when I got home. The last thing I wanted to do was go back out again! After a few times of going when I felt like that, I realized those nights God really moved among the inmates. I never let that be an excuse not to go from then on. I got excited because something good was going to happen that night, and it always did.

I had a friend come in with me for about a year or two. It was a blessing to see him minister to the inmates. It's always a blessing to help someone else fulfill their call. When we realize we, as Christians, are all in this together. Our main goal is to continue Jesus' Ministry by working together as we are one with Christ. It's not about a select few; it's about all of us being equal and submitting to Jesus' purpose!

Another experience, it took a long time to get approval to bring a book into the prison. We got the okay and the date we could take them in. The church I attended paid for them, and that day finally came. I took, I believe, 60 books into the block. The day I took them in, a man close to seven feet tall came up to me, bounced his chest off my face, and asked, "What does it take for me to get saved?" He received Jesus that day as his Lord and Savior! He showed me a hole in his leg, not healed yet, where the police shot him, to stop him, while committing a crime.

    I have experienced a lot of things that went on, and been put in tough situations, where if God doesn't speak through me, I'm shooting from the hip, but He always shows up.

 So, to say all that, and you're reading this now, and you wonder, what if I don't know what to say? God will never leave you hanging; he will put the words in your mouth. The key is to step out of your boat, and He will help you through the whole situation. That way, He and He alone will get ALL the Glory!!! The following week, when I got to the block, this new believer yelled to everyone in the block, "Get you're a$$'s in here for Bible study." A couple of guys asked me if I was going to tell him about his language. I said, he is a new believer, and we need to grace him and let God convict him. That's in God's timing, not ours, but if he asks, we must share the truth.

    I used to share from **Romans 12:1–2** often—how we are called to offer ourselves as a living sacrifice to God. As we surrender our lives, we become that sacrifice by taking up our cross daily and dying to self—our fleshly nature—so our spirit can grow strong.

When Jesus hung on the cross, He was crucifying His flesh as a sacrifice to the Father, the final offering for sin.

Verse two tells us, *"Do not be conformed to this world, but be transformed by the renewing of your mind."* The only way to renew our minds is through a daily practice of reading and applying God's Word—believing His promises even when we don't see them happening right away.

Our mind is where Satan attacks most fiercely with ungodly thoughts, and that's why it must be transformed by truth. These are powerful scriptures we studied in the block. We had some deep discussions that truly helped us grow. When two or more gather in His name, the Holy Spirit is there to bring truth and wisdom.

I only had one bad experience outside of the prison with a former inmate. We got along very well for two years while in prison. He was the guy who would invite all the inmates to come to the Bible study. I gave him my number when he was released. A month or so later, he called me about an hour before I was leaving for the prison and asked for a ride home. He was waiting outside a garage right by the prison. I told him I would be there in half an hour. I picked him up, and all he wanted was money. His voice was different, very demanding. I told him I didn't have my wallet, and he became very mad and belligerent. I reached into my pocket, pulled out a 10-dollar bill, and gave it to him. He jumped out of the car right there and left. He didn't want a ride; he just set me up to get money. I was more upset about him treating me that way and seeing him go back to probably drugs, than wanting money. I had a lot of hope that he would stay clean and live a Godly life. It could make you want to stop helping inmates, but if going in can change one person, it's worth it.

That leads to another story about a young inmate who came to the Bible study, hungry for God. He got saved and showed a lot of desire to change. I don't know how long he was there or what he did. I never ask anyone what they're in for. He was released after about six months. He showed up at our church to see me and tell me he is now a children's pastor and is doing very well. It's a blessing to see someone come out of a bad place and serve the Lord.

Something different began to happen when I entered the block: the inmates started coming up to me right away and asking questions. Most of them wouldn't come to Bible study, but had many questions about God. Also, after I came out, there they were again, like a big group, asking more questions. Those were good times. I got to answer their questions and share Scripture!

I knew, in my heart, that most people want to know about God but are afraid to ask. If we give people the opportunity and reach out to them, they will ask. The toughest people will melt when you tell them about God's love and forgiveness. You must be honest and tell them the whole truth! The guards were very willing to let me go over to their tables and let me talk. God will give you favor when you reach out in love to do His will.

Another good story: one of the inmates became a friend of mine when he was released. Came to church, met a girl, and she came to church after she got saved. About six to twelve months later, they asked me to perform their marriage. What a blessing to see them get married!

About my 7th year of teaching, one of my school students asked what I was doing that night. I told him I go to prison on Thursday nights and have a Bible study with the inmates. Almost all the students looked up and asked, "Why do you do that?" and asked us what happened. I thought, 'Yes, now I get to share' because they asked.

I explained that I am a Christian and that God put it on my heart to share Jesus in prison. So, I applied and started going every Thursday night. I told them I get to share what my life was like and how God healed me of anxiety and panic attacks. Jesus rescued me and saved me from eternity in hell. That started another subject.

So, I got to explain the whole salvation message to them, and I asked if anyone had any questions about salvation. I could talk to them now or in private. They wanted more, so I shared how to surrender their lives to God, admit they're sinners, and receive Jesus into their lives. Throughout the next five years I taught, I got to share the salvation message.

Throughout those five years, almost every Thursday, the students would ask if I was going to prison that night. Then on Friday, they asked what happened! We always had a good conversation that lasted some time. After a couple of years, I would tell the inmates how the kids were asking about them. The inmates kept telling me to tell the kids to stay away from drugs and alcohol. At times, too, inmates would tell me to tell the students to stay in school! We had so many good times talking about life, God, and the struggles teenagers go through.

One More Story.... Every year, I would ask the Lord what he wanted to work on in me, and he always answered. One year, I asked whether a chaplain's position would open for me. I believe, with all my heart, that I heard God clearly say, "You are right where I want you to be." Encouraging and pointing these students to me so they won't end up in prison! My heart sank, and I was sad about the chaplains' position, but I immediately felt peace, knowing this is where I'm supposed to be — encouraging these kids and pointing them to Jesus!

Lord, thank You for the opportunity to share the Gospel of Jesus, to encourage, and to let the inmates know that You are always there to hear their cries and save them from eternity in hell! Only one way to Heaven through Jesus! May Your Name be Glorified in every prison throughout the world!!!

CHAPTER EIGHTEEN
Mens Group

I wanted to leave this chapter for this part of the book. My prayer is for any men who have never been involved in a men's group. I want to share what happens when you get involved!

I met a man the first time I entered a church, in which I received salvation. He reached out to me and asked me if there was anything he could do for me. I was impressed and did follow up with some questions. He met with me the next Sunday, and after my questions, he recommended a Bible and how to start reading and studying God's word. We talked by phone every Sunday until we moved closer to the church about six months later.

The day we moved, we unloaded the U-Haul and left the next day to meet him and his family at a State Park, where they invited us to stay for the week. We also met another couple at the park, and we all shared a campfire for the week, and talked about Jesus! What an awesome week we had! I had no idea how Christians lived and talked until that weekend. We watched Christian videos and laughed all weekend.

We ended the weekend pumped up for Jesus. We returned home to find a beautiful picture hanging above the fireplace that read, "As for me and my house, we will serve the Lord!" Our lifelong friend surprised us with this picture! We put everything away and settled in.

My friend told me he was going to start a men's group in his old milk house. He sold his cows and fixed up the milkhouse. He wanted me to come. I jumped on that invitation. At the same time, I would go over to his farm and help him remodel the upstairs. We always ended up sharing Scriptures. Every time I have visited him, his Bible is always open on his large kitchen table.

My friend decided we would all meet every Monday at 6:00 pm. We would share our week for about ten minutes, then listen to worship songs for at least twenty minutes. He would then share a story or teaching from the Bible that brought our understanding to a level we could all relate to. To today I believe he is one of the best teachers of God's Word. We finished the night with a prayer for anyone who needed it, and for anyone we knew who did. We will finish about 9:00 pm.

Over the weeks, I have come to realize why God says not to forsake fellowship with one another. We can learn and worship together in a church setting, but nothing beats getting together with other men—or, for women, other women. God knows exactly what we need, and you can't share some things with men and women together; there is a place for that!

I will never forget the night we talked about some of the struggles men have. I was so excited to hear that most men struggle with the same desires. You will only hear that in a group of men who are open with each other. I'm writing to glorify God and to encourage men who may be reading to get involved in a men's group. Looking back, I honestly don't know where I would be without these men who encouraged me.

Another Story: My wife and I went through some tough times in our marriage after we got saved. We saw a couple of different counselors over two years. These men stood by me, and their wives stood by my wife. I believe with all my heart that if you're in that position, you need brothers or sisters to stand with you. Make sure they're not going to say negative things about your spouse; speak life into your marriage, not death!!! Too many marriages fall apart because your friends speak negatively about your marriage rather than toward restoration. Restoration is God's way. He said, "What God puts together, let no man separate!" Negativity breeds death in marriages!

Our marriage was restored, and I thank God and all the people who stood with us until it was restored. One couple found out I had lost my wedding ring, bought me a new one, and we renewed our vows on our 25th Wedding Anniversary! Praise God for men and women who stand on His Word to the end! This is a result of surrendering to God's plan, never forsaking fellowship!

One time, we prayed for a little girl that the doctor told her parents to abort. They said she will not make it. We, along with some other believers, prayed, and that little girl was born healthy and fine. Praise God. We have experienced many healings and salvations from praying and believing with others.

The greatest thing was that all twelve of us were discipled for many years, and some moved into ministry. We all received the Baptism of the Holy Spirit and were on fire for God.

I want to thank You, Lord, and our lifelong friend, who spent countless hours pouring into many men with all his heart! Lord, none of this could have been done without Your love for all Your Creation.

This is a must: **Matthew 28:19** — Jesus said, *"Go make disciples of all nations, baptizing them in the name of the Father and the Son and the Holy Spirit!"*

Thank You again, Lord, for putting us all together and for becoming disciples of You, Lord, in Jesus' Name!

CHAPTER NINETEEN
Retired and Moved Again

I had my second knee replacement in September of 2018 and retired from the Career Center on January 1, 2019. That summer, I left the prison position and went with a friend of ours to start a church. His goal was to have church on Thursday night, but after eight months, he resigned. Sherri and I took over and pastored the church. We had services on Sundays for about one and a half years.

We had about 20 people start with us, and we had services every Sunday. We also had a discipleship class one hour before service every week. My wife and I cleaned the church every week before the service. Sherri did worship, and we had a service every Sunday Morning. We really thought this was going to grow, but tragedy struck our family.

Our Grandson and his fiancée were killed in a motorcycle accident shortly after we started. We were all devastated!! My wife and my daughter were talking about us moving up by them. We wanted to move, but we wanted what God wanted.

So, I put out a fleece and God answered it in 15 minutes or less. In the Bible, Gideon put out a fleece before God to seek confirmation of God's will – see **Judges 6:36-40.** I immediately asked God to forgive me because it was too fast, and I wanted to make sure He said, "move." So, I was in a pizza shop in our small town, and I heard the young lady talking to a gentleman about cleaning a house. Their conversation sounded like she might have been a realtor. I asked her if she was, and she said yes. I explained that we might want to sell our home.

Making a long story short, she came out to the house about a week later. She looked it over and gave us a price about three days later. She said it's taking around six months to sell in our area. So, I put out another fleece. I asked the Lord if He really wanted us to move and leave the church, since it would be over 100 miles away. We signed papers the next day. The following day, the owner of the realty came with about eight workers to go through the house. That morning, our daughter found a house she thought we would like, so we drove up to see it. We liked the house and made an offer that night. That same night we got home, the realtor called and said we needed to meet tomorrow morning before 9:00. The realtor came over and said, "Your House is sold!" We were in shock!!! They wanted to move in in three weeks. We called a moving company to move us after we packed up everything. We had to tell the church that we are moving and were helped with the transition.

Two days before the signing date, we finalized everything, but the buyers changed the date. What a mess —the moving company had no time available to move us now. I called my previous Pastor, with whom I kept in close touch, and he said he would have help there in the morning. So, we rented a U-Haul, and about 12 guys showed up the next morning and had us loaded in a half hour. What a Blessing they all were!

 When you're in a problem you see no way out, the Lord has a way out, no matter what the situation — help, sin, anger, fear. He is always there to provide!!! That's why we build a relationship with God. He wants to be a part of your whole life, not just on Sunday, and that's why we worship Him all day!!!

We arrived at our new house, and my brother-in-law helped me move until my son-in-law finished unloading. My brother-in-law was a strong man, but he was having some trouble; he didn't know he was full of cancer. He would give you the shirt off his back for anyone.

When we got to our new place in Pittsfield, I must be honest, it was a heartache for both of us! We left a lot of lifetime friends, a church, and our lifestyle of 64 years. We unloaded and put everything away in our new home. We liked the location, and having a 2-car garage was a blessing! It's been a real Blessing because we are only 12 miles from our daughter's house.

Our daughter recommended the Free Methodist Church near our house instead of the one where she attended. We attended the Free Methodist Church that Sunday. We knew immediately, this is where we belong. We became members that first month. I began attending a Tuesday night prayer meeting and was shocked to see that there were more men than women. Every prayer meeting I was ever at, the women outnumbered the men two to one.

The Pastor was excellent at relating to people. We've met quite a few friends with whom we go motorcycle riding. We got involved in a house group with friends we met at the YMCA. It's been a real Blessing. I asked one assistant Pastor if they pray for the Pastor before the service on Sunday. She said, they don't, but would ask the Pastor if we could. She told me a week later, the Pastor would like that. We now pray every Sunday before the service, and the Pastor calls it the Upper Room. The Lord shows up every time we meet. I always believed Pastors are on the front lines in the church and always need prayers from the church body!

COVID hit, and the church worshipped online until May. The Pastor said, "I'm opening the church, it will be open to worship our God!" The church filled up and grew every month. People put their trust in God, not man! Pastor made it clear, if you're not comfortable coming yet, that's ok! He still has the service on live every week, for those who can't make it.

The church feeds up to 200 people every week for the community! They take food to the poor every week and reach out spiritually as they deliver it. This is a church that is being the hands and feet of God!

The men in the church cut the five acres of grass every week in summer and do all the upkeep. The men are constantly remodeling and repairing the church, all with free labor. The Pastor is there every day, working late hours. What an Awesome church in a small town!!! We can get together more often now with our family and help them during the loss of their precious son. I got involved in subbing at a High School in the area, and Sherri cleans houses at times.

We got involved in a house group that meets every week except in the summer. The house group is run by an awesome couple who give all of themselves to help and disciple Christians. No matter where they go, they are sharing Jesus!

I started a men's group to encourage and disciple men, with the hope of eventually having them form their own group to disciple. I believe many believers were never discipled, and the result is some falling away from the faith, because it's more than just going to church; it's a whole new life. The Bible says we are a new creation when we are born again. Our new life replaces our old way of living and our desires.

I get to preach occasionally at a church about 50 miles away to fill in until they get a full-time pastor. It is rewarding to encourage believers I have never met before. I'm starting to feel like we belong there. It is a small country church, and the people are very respectful and love God. They treat my wife and me as if they had known us our whole lives.

My wife and I are very Blessed to live where we do now. For our entire lives, we have loved the same hobbies. We enjoy riding motorcycles, which she also always had her own. We love riding bicycles, going for walks, and enjoying being outside until dark. We love to spend time with family and friends. The area we live in now offers the best of everything we like to enjoy. Another one of our favorite things to do is help others in need, whether cutting grass, helping around the house, visiting, and sharing the love of JESUS WITH THEM. If we see a need, we will help them!

CHAPTER TWENTY
Surprise Blessing from God

Sherri and I had the opportunity to visit Florida for one week during the winter. We loved it because of the weather, and I suffer from arthritis in my back, neck, and hands. We like to ride bicycles, and there are many miles of golf cart and bicycle trails. The following year, the park changed its rules, and no one could rent. We found a place in another park for one month.

We drove through the first park one day and found a beautiful place for sale for $3000. Equivalent to others selling for $20,000. New roof, plumbing, bathroom, and 12x16 family room. We bought it immediately from another Christian family who became close friends. They bought a newer park model in the park. Never did we think we would have an opportunity like this in our lives, but GOD! He provided a way again!

We met people we were friends with back home in New Wilmington, PA. They became friends, we went to church with them, and met for a bike ride and picnic every week while in Florida.

One night, while attending a Bible study in Florida, we met a 79-year-old lady who was also from Pennsylvania. She had just lost her husband and grandson, and something was said in the Bible study that triggered the grief in her heart, and she ran outside. After the meeting, we encouraged her and walked home together. From then on, we became good friends and even today call her Mom. We still call her Mom because she said I look like her son. Sherri and I visit her house during the summer to do some work and play games. There is also a beautiful bike trail there that we ride while we visit her, just as we do in Florida.

I am Blessed to say that we have celebrated our 51st anniversary and have learned, with the help of the Lord Jesus, to love each other much more than when we first got married. I believe the key to a good marriage is to follow the Bible and what JESUS TAUGHT! Put each other ahead of yourself. Jump in and do dishes when you can, maybe do the washing. There are always ways to bless your spouse by sharing the load. Always pray for the best for them! Never talk badly about them to someone else. Remember the Bible says, we are one in the flesh. So, if we fight with them, we fight against ourselves! Always make a date with them each week if you can. Look for what makes them happy and surprise them with it. Remember, this goes both ways!

Remember to always put Jesus first in your life!

About David

Life brings all different kinds of troubles, but God has all the answers! Press into His Word and you will discover truth.

David Bartholomew is very outgoing with people. He loves God, people, and family. If you make eye contact with him, he probably will come up to you and ask how you're doing. He loves to share how much Jesus loves you. Do you need prayer?

He loves the outdoors, hunting, fishing, campfires, riding bicycles, and motorcycles. He loves working with wood and doing small construction jobs for people. Most of all, he wrote this book so people who struggle with life could be led to the truth, Jesus. He also likes to disciple people and help them learn the truth because if you don't get discipled, you may fall away from salvation.

www.ingramcontent.com/pod-product-compliance
Lightning Source LLC
Chambersburg PA
CBHW021024090426
42738CB00007B/892